Communication policies in Hungary

In this series

Communication policies in **Hungary**

by Tamás Szecskő and Gábor Fodor

The Unesco Press
Paris 1974

Published by The Unesco Press,
7 Place de Fontenoy, 75700 Paris
Printed by Imprimerie Aubin, 86240 Ligugé (7657)

ISBN 92-3-101154-5
French edition 92-3-201154-9

Preface

Communication policies are sets of principles and norms established to guide the behaviour of communication systems. They are shaped over time in the context of society's general approach to communication and to the media. Emanating from political ideologies, the social and economic conditions of the country and the values on which they are based, they strive to relate these to the real needs for and the prospective opportunities of communication.

Communication policies exist in every society, though they may sometimes be latent and disjointed, rather than clearly articulated and harmonized. They may be very general, in the nature of desirable goals and principles, or they may be more specific and practically binding. They may exist or be formulated at many levels. They may be incorporated in the constitution or legislation of a country; in over-all national policies, in the guidelines for individual administrations, in professional codes of ethics as well as in the constitutions and operational rules of particular communication institutions.

The publication of this series of studies has been undertaken as part of the programme adopted by the General Conference of Unesco at its sixteenth session, related to the analysis of communication policies as they exist at the different levels—public, institutional, professional—in selected countries. The aim of the series is to present this information in a manner which can be comparable. Thus an attempt has been made to follow, as far as possible, a fairly similar structural pattern and method of approach which was agreed between the national institutions undertaking the work.

This survey of communication policies in Hungary was written by Tamás Szecskő and Gábor Fodor from the Mass Communication Research Centre of the Hungarian Radio and Television. The opinions expressed by the authors do not necessarily reflect the views of Unesco.

Contents

Contents

1 Mass communication—policies—planning

If we conceive policies—whether they be economic, cultural or strictly communication policies—merely as mechanisms for decision-making, for the execution of those decisions, and for control of such execution, the task of presenting them is fairly easy: since it would call only for a listing and description of already existing and functioning institutions and processes. The task is different if we use a more complex interpretation of policies. In this case the concepts of value and value-orientation also come under examination, either when we attempt to place given decisions within the frame of reference of the social system of values, or when we trace back various policies to the politics of power relations, meeting again with the concepts of value, of historical alternatives, and of the teleology of social activity.

Yet we cannot but choose the latter way, taking the risk that at times our thinking will oscillate half-way between 'what is' and 'what ought to be', at the intersection of present and future social conditions. The subject itself induces us to adopt this latter method, since the common handling of communication planning necessitates—even on the level of description—the adoption of a 'policy-oriented' conception of social research. We do not deem this approach enriched with elements of value and interest at all alien to the scientific method, since we are convinced that in our age one of the most important 'subversive factors' of social structures and processes is science itself.

Before entering into detail, it seems necessary to define how we shall here understand 'mass communication'; what is the place of the mass communication system within the broader range of institutions of social communication; to what extent the structure and functions of mass communication are influenced by the new type of socialist society that is being built up in Hungary; how shall we interpret the concept of 'policies', and what link there is between policies and politics on the one hand and policies and planning on the other.

Mass communication is a form of social communication and is quite distinct from either personal, or inter-group communication. Its three important characteristics are: massiveness, heterogeneity and use of technical media.

Mass communication processes are massive in three respects, first they convey information, culture, entertainment in massive quantities; secondly, these are received by masses of the public; and thirdly, the technical-technological process of 'manufacturing', 'producing' the communication contents, can be compared to a certain extent to the technological process of industrial mass production. Mass communication is heterogeneous both as regards contents, and public: its communications are different as to quality, form, system of coding and function; it addresses itself to members of all the different social classes, at various cultural levels in various spheres of interest and ways of life. The sender of the message, the communicator, has no relation with the recipient, because a technical medium or, rather, a techno-logical chain is interposed: composing-machine, rotary press, microphone, camera, studio installations, amplifiers, transmitters and receivers.

Definitions in the literature often emphasize the point that in the mass communication process the emitter is, as a rule, not an individual, but a social institution; that the flow of messages is mainly one-way, i.e. the communicator usually has the talking role; that the act of reception takes place simultaneously with the emission, or after a brief time lag. These features, however, are only of relative validity and they are for the most part already implicit in the factors referred to previously.

A much more important feature, and this is emphatically set forth in Hungarian research, is the historical character of mass communication. Processes of mass communication stemmed from the first industrial revolution simultaneously with capitalist mass production, and became the most charac-teristic subsystem of social communication by the twentieth century. In both the capitalist and socialist types of societies of the economically developed world, they bear in their structure and functioning the historical marks peculiar to the given society. All this leads, among others, to a rather important conclusion: it cannot be proved that, taking a long enough perspec-tive, the decline of commodity production will not lead necessarily to a disorganization of the mass communication system in today's sense, reflecting in part market conditions.

In every society the mass communication system fits organically into both the political system and the system of educational and cultural institu-tions.

We shall make a few comments on the diagram, or rather on the relations between the mass communication system and other social institutions as they are interpreted in Hungarian research work and in the communicators' practice:

Given the mass appeal of its content, the size of its public, and its ability to reach quickly, mass communication offers the most flexible system of political and cultural media which the ruling classes in all advanced societies have used as an instrument of political power.

Because of its direct political importance and as a force favouring integration, adaptation and socialization, mass communication is directed and oriented in every organized society—differences between societies being evident only in methods and forms of regulation.

Integration of the mass communication system into the systems of political and cultural institutions of the society makes it obvious that the optimal influence of mass communication can be exerted only in parallel with

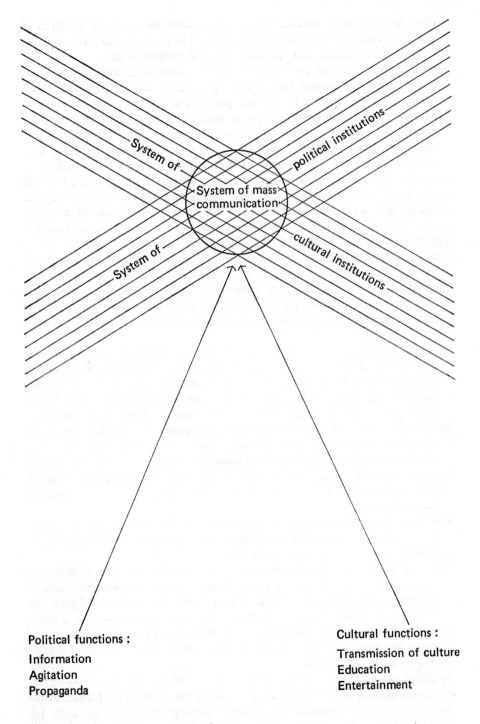

Political functions :
Information
Agitation
Propaganda

Cultural functions :
Transmission of culture
Education
Entertainment

FIG. 1. System of mass communication

11

these socio-cultural systems for effective performance of the function of mass influence and transmission of culture. The mass media must co-operate with the other media and channels of social communication.

The difference between the functions of the mass communication systems are relative: information has aspects of agitation and propaganda, entertainment may help—or block—the possibilities of spreading culture, etc. Moreover, the two basic groups of functions are also overlapping: the general activity of cultural transmission influences the possibilities and outcome of political influence and, in turn, political mass influence may help or hinder the effectiveness of processes of cultural transmission.

Since the Hungarian mass communication system is being formed within a new type or socialist society, it has some characteristics both as regards structure and its functions which are either new or prevail to a higher degree than in the mass communication systems of non-socialist societies. The more important of these are the following:

The basic model of socialist mass communication—the Bolshevik party press—which had been involved in political activity since its creation and enriched by the revolutionary experience of the international working-class movement, became the organizational pattern for the mass communication system of the new society in socialist countries of Europe—among them Hungary.

Since this society involves the planning of the most important social processes, the system of mass communication and that of political and cultural institutions can be more fully and methodically integrated. This is due partly to the integrated character of social planning and partly to the fact that no single element of mass communication is privately owned.

In this new type of mass communication system the market forces do not play a determining role, therefore application of the principle of the 'lowest common denominator' traditionally characteristic of the system, can be limited. This is to be seen in the 'stratum-orientation' which is found in the socialist systems far more than in traditional mass communication systems.

This type of mass communication has a definitely historical character: present events are not considered to be of interest in themselves but rather in their relation to the past or to the future.

Since this is a society quasi 'on the way', a transitional society, whose people, after a political revolution, are living through revolutionary transformations of their culture and way of life, and in which the elements of past and present are combined, mass communication must necessarily play a larger part in the process of socialization—in making the new social values and norms accepted—and also, in reflecting the conflicting values characteristic of a transitional period.

By policies—whether economic, cultural or communication policies—we understand orders of preference regarding social goals. Policies are formed within the wider frame of reference of politics, selecting and specifying aims and principles for given fields of social activity, roughly outlining also the ways leading to the preferred aims. For each field of activity the system of management is differently conceived[1]:[1] it includes all the mechanisms by which the given field—economy, culture, communication—functions and also the means by which society or some of its organs, e.g. government, can influence this functioning. (A given policy may prevail in several systems of management, as has been the case in the past decade in the Hungarian national economy.) Finally the plan lays down the actual goals of a period and also the means and method to be used to achieve those aims. In working out plans an important role is played—in addition to the above factors—by the alternatives revealed by forecasts, since one of the future variants will become the basis of the plan[2].

Thus, if the present monograph is to describe the operating principles of mass communication in Hungary, it cannot be confined to the presentation of communication 'policies' as indicated by the title, but must also outline the mechanism of the management and operation of the mass communication system, as well as the planning of mass communication. We shall concentrate here primarily on the functions of the press, radio and television, and only where necessary shall we mention other means of mass communication or the social communication system other than the mass communication media.

The film industry, record production and book publishing, for example, are sometimes included in the system of mass communication as far as the technical aspects of their activities are concerned. Communication policies, however, do not relate to them in general: under Hungarian socio-political conditions they are mainly influenced by cultural policies both on national and organizational levels. This explains the very brief treatment to be given here of these cultural institutions of first importance.

1. Figures in brackets refer to the notes on pages 55-56.

2 Historical development of mass communication system

Press historians consider *Mercurius Hungaricus,* published in Latin between 1705 and 1710, as the first appearance of mass communication in Hungary. It may be taken as symbolic that this first Hungarian newspaper was born as an organ in support of a war of independence: its aim was to give authentic information to European readers on the war led by Ferenc Rákóczi II against the Hapsburgs, arguing against the *Wienerisches Diarium* which abused Rákóczi and his soldiers.

The first newspaper in the Hungarian language, *Magyar Hirmondó* (Hungarian Courier), was published as late as 1780, taking advantage of the possibilities accorded by the liberal administration of Emperor Joseph II. In the age of enlightenment several Hungarian-language journals appeared and, although most of them were published in Vienna and Pozsony, they helped greatly to inform the progressive strata of Hungarian nobility and citizenry about the revolutionary changes in West European political and cultural life. The first Hungarian periodical, *Magyar Muzeum* (Hungarian Museum), published in 1788, and other later periodicals contributed, together with the newspapers, to strengthening Hungarian national consciousness, and fostering and developing Hungarian literature.

In the first two decades of the nineteenth century the ebb of the European revolutionary movements, the supression of the Martinovits conspiracy against the Hapsburgs—a movement of Hungarian intellectual circles— followed by an imposition of censorship set back the development of the political press, a relatively smooth existence being assured only for periodicals and the literary annuals. But the thirties, the so-called 'Age of Reforms' gave a new impetus to the Hungarian political press. The beginnings of Hungarian industry, the remarkably quick development of *bourgeois* civilization and the establishment of political institutions in the fight for independence provided the conditions favourable to strengthening the role of the press in the forming of public opinion and the development of ideologies. *Orszaggyülési Tudósitások* (Parliamentary Information) edited by Lajos Kossuth, the publication of *Pesti Hirlap* (News of Pest), the journal of the reform politician Count István Széchenyi, *Jelenkor* (Present Age), and various short-lived newspapers all gave evidence that the fight for *bourgeois* development and national independence rendered the press an integral part of the political system. A new form of mass communication appeared also at that time, the so-called 'fashion journals', which published literature and critiques, patronized the fast developing Hungarian Literature and in addition printed fashion pictures which helped the journals to reach further strata of the reading public.

One of the first achievements of the 1848 *bourgeois* revolution was the abolishment of censorship, the establishment of the free press. Act XVIII of 1848 which regulated the activities of the press was drawn up on the basis of the press law of the July Monarchy of France, and of the Belgian press law. It lays down that 'everybody is free to publish and spread their thoughts through the press', but at the same time the publication licence of a journal was bound to a rather large deposit. Agitation for forced change of religion or of the constitution, high treason and abuse were considered offences against press laws, and the declaration of such was remitted to the jury, on Western examples. This act was valid until 1914. Then the government, preparing for the war, introduced several modifications—obligation to publish corrections, compensations, restriction of the journalist's right to plead in case of libel suits, etc.—in order to facilitate control of the opposition press.

After the Hungarian parliament had accepted, and the king sanctioned the new press law, a revolutionary development started in the Hungarian press. While before March 1848 a total of thirty-three Hungarian-language and nineteen German-language journals were published in the country, within a short time after introduction of the new law eighty-six new periodical publications in Hungarian and foreign languages began to circulate. The methods of distribution had also changed: in the streets of Pest and Buda newsmen appeared selling the new paper of the revolutionary youth, *March 15th*. Another new feature of mass communication was the development of a new type of journal, the papers of mass circulation. The *Nép Barátja* (Friend of the People) addressed to peasants and published also in the languages of minorities living in Hungary, and the radical *Munkások Ujsága* (Labourers' Journal) were intended for social strata which no newspapers had reached before the revolution.

Defeat in the war of independence entailed, of course, a setback in the development of the press. Only nine journals survived out of those published during the revolution. The period between the war of independence and the Compromise of 1867 was, as regards the press, one of stagnation, but this was the time when the elements of technical infrastructure necessary for later development began to emerge. In 1849 railways in Hungary covered only 178 kilometres, but by 1866 this had increased to 2,000 kilometres, thus enabling the distribution of journals by mail, and a faster flow of information between Vienna and Pest-Buda and the provinces which was essential for the development of the local press.

The fever of railway building which rose even higher after 1867 was the first sign of the accelerating economic development, which was to mark the last decades of the nineteenth century and the turn of the century. This retarded development, which followed West European development with a 50–100 years delay, entailed an upswing of the urbanization process, accelerated social mobility and, of course, had its effect on the development of the mass communication system. Although quite a considerable proportion of the population was illiterate, by the first years of the twentieth century Hungary was among the leading European nations with regard to the press. In 1867, 119 periodical publications were published; in 1900, more than 1,000; and in 1906, 1,787 with a total number of copies amounting to 160 million. In Budapest readers could buy thirty different dailies in the Hungarian language, and nine dailies in German, while in London there appeared twenty-five dailies, in Vienna twenty-four, and in Rome fourteen. The number of copies per head was also higher here than in England, and three times as high as in Russia or Serbia.

In the early years of the twentieth century the Hungarian press also made enormous technical progress. From the beginning of the century until the outbreak of the First World War the number of printing houses in Hungary had grown threefold, and the number of qualified printworkers had doubled. The first modern caster was installed in 1900, and by the end of the year 20 were already in operation, and by 1914 their number had reached 216. Fast technical development, and growing competition accelerated, of course, concentration of the large-scale printing industry, and this had its reaction on the press: vertical mergers of publishing companies and printing houses became customary[3].

Between the Compromise of 1867 and the First World War the first cheap large-circulation daily papers appeared in Hungary, based mainly on advertisements, and the first sensational newspapers. Since this was a period of dynamic development of the fairly new Hungarian capitalism, the importance of the working class was also growing quickly as was its organization. This called forth the first workers' journals: *Arany-trombita* (Golden Trumpet) edited by Mihály Táncsics, the *Általános Munkás Ujság* (Universal Workers' Newspaper), the *Munkás Heti Krónika* (Workers' Weekly Chronicle), published in Hungarian and German, and later *Népszava* (The People's Voice), the central organ of the Party of Social Democrats.

The *bourgeois* revolution of 1918, the so-called 'Michaelmas Daisy' revolution, abolished the restricting regulations of the war years and established the necessary legal basis for the freedom of the press. The left-wing press was strengthening in number and in authority: the social democrats and the trade unions founded several new, mainly local newspapers, and the first communist journal appeared, the *Vörös Ujság* (Red Journal), soon followed by other journals directed towards the various social strata: peasants, soldiers and youth.

In 1919, after proclamation of the Hungarian Soviet Republic, the management of the press was put into the hands of the Press Directorate, appointed by the government. This organ of the proletarian revolution had the task of abolishing some of the hostile *bourgeois* journals and starting new journals (during the few months of the proletarian dictatorship more than 500 periodical publications appeared), of distributing the scarce paper supply and acting as the policy-making body for the press.

In the communist press of the first Hungarian proletarian dictatorship the dilemma—ever since one of the fundamental problems of communist mass communication—already appeared: what should be the relation of the press to social policies, that is, how many critical elements are to be involved in the freedom of the press in the communist sense under the conditions of building the new society. One of the most explicit answers to the question at the time—reflecting largely the Leninist conception of the press—was the following:

The task of the press and criticism is not only to praise the revolution and, faced with the troubles, crises and poverty of the transition period, to show only the beautiful outlines of the new world which is being built, but also, to point out defects, as well as progress. Negligence, disorder, destruction must be condemned. Stupidities, errors inherited from the old order must be unmasked. Instead of banal glorification, actual facts must be brought to light. These are the tasks of the press and criticism in the proletarian state [4].

After the defeat of the Hungarian Soviet Republic the government introduced prior censorship, in an attempt to reduce to a minimum the living space of the left-wing press. The whole of the communist press was forced underground, but the press of the social democrats and of the trade unions also had its losses. The composition of the *bourgeois* press underwent a definite change, the proportion of right-wing journals—from 1932 openly fascist—was growing constantly. The great upswing and cosmopolitan orientation of the *bourgeois* press broke down before the First World War, and Hungarian mass communication became very provincial. Consecutive governments each shifted further to the right than the preceding one and 'purification' took place among journals and journalists on several occasions. Only two of the traditional daily papers—with the exception of government organs—survived the last one, which followed the German occupation in March 1944.

As in most countries of Europe, broadcasting was started and grew apace in the period between the two world wars. (However, as early as 1893, the forerunner of the radio, a 'telephone news' service, was in fact operating although the number of its subscribers was never more than 9,000, not even in 1930 when its development was at the peak.) When, on 1 December 1925, the official inaugural radio concert was performed, the number of subscribers was 10,000. In 1934 the new, powerful transmitter at Lakihegy was built and a second programme could be added to the first. Strangely enough, in 1938 the number of subscribers was only 419,000, indicating a very slow progress. The *Radio News* of the period wrote:

. . . instead of further progress, we have to face symptoms of a slow but steady decline . . . farmers making up more than half of the earning population are unable to become listeners in the sixteenth year of broadcasting and according to data put at our disposal the number of receivers meeting the educational demands of an agrarian population of 3 million, is less than 20,000. While in this twentieth century the highest treasures of science, arts and high-level entertainment are broadcast over the air and also the news of most events, none of this can reach the agricultural population and they cannot be informed [5].

17

In the years of the Second World War, during the anti-facist fighting, the underground papers issued by the Communist Party—like *Szabad Nép* (Free People)—played a very important role, as did *Népszava* (The People's Voice: Social Democratic), and as long as they were not suspended, *Magyar Nemzet* (Hungarian People), *Szabad Szó* (Free Voice) and among the Monday papers the *Független Magyarország* (Independent Hungary).

After the Second World War the social revolution transformed almost all social, economic and political structures and at the same time radically reorganized the structure of mass communication.

While creating better material conditions for education, the technical facilities of mass communication were taken over by public ownership thus establishing the right conditions for the freedom of the press reflecting the idea of Saint Just characteristic of every revolutionary dictatorship since the great French Revolution: 'Freedom for all but not for the enemies of freedom.'

3 Social structure— communication structure

The political framework of the mass communication system in Hungary is the socialist system, its economic framework is public ownership of the means of production, the cultural and educational institutions, and the information media; while its legal framework is the right to information and freedom of speech.

In the past twenty-five years as a consequence of the abolition of exploitation, Hungarian society has shown a very high level of social mobility: hundreds of thousands have moved from one region of the country to another, directed from the 'peripheries' towards the centres; hundreds of thousands have abandoned their former activities, their social group, stratum and class to give a new sense to their life and work in a new environment and a new social structure. Large-scale mobility is necessarily accompanied by an impressive process of urbanization. In some Hungarian towns the population has increased tenfold in twenty years, and traditional villages are being penetrated by modern, 'urban', industrial value systems to a growing extent.

The data of the latest census—in 1970—demonstrate the above trends of social development in several respects of which we shall illustrate two tendencies (see Tables 1 and 2).

TABLE 1. Percentage territorial distribution of the population in Hungary [6]

Year	Budapest	Other towns	Villages	Year	Budapest	Other towns	Villages
1930	16.6	21.5	61.9	1960	18.8	26.3	58.4
1949	17.3	21.1	61.6	1970	18.1	23.5	54.9

Approached from another angle, the proportion of manpower engaged in farming has markedly decreased, even within the structure of material production (see Table 2).

As seen also from the above data, a change has taken place in the structure of Hungarian economy in the past twenty-five years. The complex process of socialist industrialization resulted in the creation of new branches of industry, new factories and jobs equally also in the territorial restructurization of productive activities, reducing—though not yet eliminating—the excessive Budapest orientation of Hungarian economic life.

TABLE 2. The distribution of active earners (percentage) by branches of the national economy [7]

Branch	1960	1970	Branch	1960	1970
Industry	28	37	Transport and communication	6	7
Building industry	6	7	Trade	6	8
Agriculture, forestry and water economy	39	26	Services, etc.	15	15

Last but not least, this quarter of a century has witnessed an educational 'explosion'; illiteracy, rather widespread before the war, was considerably reduced by closing the gap between the centres and peripheries of culture, and by developing a social atmosphere in which—as supported by the findings of several sociological surveys—knowledge, education, learning have taken a high rank in the scale of social values.

In 1949, 4.8 per cent of the population above the age of 10 had no schooling at all; in 1930 the percentage was 9.3, while the proportion was 1.8 per cent in 1970. On the other hand, the proportion of those who had a secondary education had increased from 5.5 to 15 per cent and the number of college and university graduates rose from 1.7 to 4.3 per cent in the period between 1943 and 1970[8].

The result of these revolutionary changes affecting almost every sphere of social life was that Hungary, although only among the middle ranks of the economically developed nations, has rated high in culture and education as shown by the relative international indices. The aggregate 'cultural index' computed according to the methodology of Unesco puts Hungary between France and the Netherlands on the scale of European nations, even though the *per capita* gross national product in these two countries is almost double that in Hungary[9].

Social ownership and the abolition of exploitation and the related socio-economic processes have changed the class structure of Hungarian society: the bases of class antagonisms have been removed but, naturally, without eliminating the existence of social classes and strata. Hungarian society is stratified and this fact has its consequences in the transmission of culture and in the communication system.

The most definite criterion of stratification in present-day Hungary is the place of the individual in the social division of labour. Depending on whether he or she is an engineer or a farmer, a teacher in a country town, a worker in a factory or a mother doing her household tasks, not only income differs but—among others—the degree of cultural consumption and the patterns of use of mass media also differ.

In the mid-sixties the cultural standards of various social groups were measured by an aggregate index of the educational level of the family members, and of their media exposure. Taking the social average as 100, the index for executives and professionals was 193; at the other extreme, the cultural level of farmers was 60, while the range for different groups of workers was rather wide: from 110 for skilled workers to 67 for unskilled workers[10].

Different strata of the population use the channels of communication in different ways. There are strata in which events of some importance are conveyed by several sources, other strata have to be satisfied with fewer channels and rather scanty information. Passing from the best educated, the socially and politically most active strata having the highest standards of living to the strata shown by social-economic indices as the least favourably situated, the number of sources of communication used by the various strata is seen to diminish gradually. In the first strata, organizational communication, the press, television and mouth-to-mouth communication—including rumour —appear together; this composite means of communication is used by the strata in the most favourable social-economic position: politically active skilled workers in urban areas, professionals, employees. The next block includes only the press, television, radio and rumour, while the third consists of the two electronic media and rumour, the fourth of radio and rumour, and finally the fifth is composed solely of rumour, the eternal, pre-industrial form of social communication. Of course, only a marginal part of the adult Hungarian population is satisfied by this lowest grade of communication, according to several surveys possibly 4 to 5 per cent, for the most part elderly people living in small villages or in scattered settlements. The bulk of the population is exposed to the communication channels described in the three intermediate blocks. However, parallel with social restratification, a certain restratification of information-seeking can be observed, by which society as a whole is climbing from level to level.

In three national sample surveys those who stated that they were exposed each day to the news given by press, radio and television were put into the category of 'maximum news consumers'; those who did not consume media news of any kind were called 'isolated'; the remainder were considered as 'moderate news consumers'. Some statistics on the three categories follow[11]:

	1966 (N=820) %	1968 (N=937) %	1969 (N=908) %
Maximum news consumers	21	33	35
Moderate news consumers	73	62	60
Isolated	6	5	5
TOTAL	100	100	100

Given the differences in degree of exposure to the media, some strata use more social news and information than others. An even more important consequence is that the social information received by the various strata also differs in quality and validity. A professional or a qualified trade union worker moves in another sphere of communication and tries to match information coming from mass communication media against that from organizational sources; he is able to seek out more information than a worker or employee dependent exclusively on the information supply of mass communication. And again in quite a different setting is the elderly farmer who is informed about what is going on in the world through rumour only. In this whole context, paradoxically enough it is the very people whose socio-economic position is least favourable and who are the most poorly educated who would need sound information, to be digested slowly, and readily available repeatedly. Yet, it is just these people who have to consume the most ephemeral forms of information calling for the most elaborate skill in processing and most exposed to various kinds of distortion. These people are, in fact, the heaviest consumers of the most volatile contents of television, radio and mouth-to-mouth communication.

Social stratification—in addition to delimiting the field of activity of mass communication in the manner described—has an influence upon Hungarian communication policies in two respects at least.

First, the structure of mass communication reflects a balance of mass and stratum-oriented information. The individual media, in their editorial policies also, pay attention to this kind of balance. This effort corresponds to the dialectics of agitation and propaganda, agitation being addressed to the general masses, while propaganda is political communication addressed to the more homogeneous strata[12].

Secondly, conflicting interests of social strata find expression in mass communication itself. This fact is stressed in a working document of the Association of Hungarian Journalists, as follows:

. . . the society of transition unites specific contradictions also in our country: its character is no longer antagonistic but in some respects it is strongly stratified, and is therefore sometimes divided by contradictions among the different strata and groups. The fundamental common interests which laid down the objective bases of socialist national unity do not exclude conflicts. The structure of mass communication, conditioned by the material parameters of the society, by the demands, processes and conflicts of development can be made up to date, can be brought closer to our objectives, if—first of all—we emphasize its primary task of representing the global interests of society as a whole, while, at the same time, we try to make it more suitable for expressing this specific kind of stratification. That is, to spread and strengthen understanding as regards the most important goals and ideals of the society, and on this basis to articulate class, stratum and group interests in order to confront them with other interests. This is one of the 'conditio sine qua non'-s of easing tensions, of perceiving and softening friction and conflicts [13].

The traditional basis of the Hungarian mass communication system is the whole of the printed press: dailies, factory newspapers, political mass circulation papers and technical journals for smaller special interest groups. A considerable part of the population reads newspapers regularly; circulation of dailies amounts to one copy for four people. In 1971, 29 dailies, 138 weeklies and fortnightlies and 318 periodicals were issued, representing a total of 1,127 million copies. Circulation of daily papers increased by about

50 per cent in the period 1961-71. During this period circulation indices of national dailies remained practically unchanged, while those of local (county and city) papers increased rapidly. The money spent *per capita* on papers more than doubled in ten years, and is about twice the amount spent on books.

On 31 December 1972, the *Hungarian Post* registered more than 2.5 million radio and more than 2 million television subscribers. On a national level this means 76 radio[14] and 62 television licences per hundred families. This average means in Budapest 85, in country towns 79, in villages 69 radio subscriptions per hundred families. The corresponding figures for television are: 69 in Budapest, 69 in country towns, 55 in villages. In 1972 the three national stations of the Hungarian Radio broadcast more than 320 hours weekly, not including the daily 1-2 hour programmes of five local stations.

In its first and second (experimental) programme the Hungarian Television transmitted fifty-four hours weekly partly in colour. The distribution by content of the two central AM programmes, in 1972, was as follows: light music, 37 per cent; classical music, 20 per cent; political programmes, 20 per cent; arts and entertainment, 13 per cent; education, 3 per cent; sports, 3 per cent; other, 4 per cent. The distribution of television programmes in 1971 was: political, 27 per cent; cultural programmes, 14 per cent; light entertainment, 41 per cent; education, 15 per cent; children's and youth programmes, 3 per cent.

Audience research has shown that the effective use of radio programmes (i.e. the quotient of actual listening time and programme hours) is 10 per cent for radio and about 40 per cent for television. Although the size of radio audiences has considerably decreased as a result of television there are still radio programmes that attract 30–40 per cent of the radio-television audience. When the most popular programmes are on the air 80–90 per cent of television sets are on. Since there are not two separate organizations for radio and television, Hungarian Radio and Television is the mass communication institution having the widest range in this country.

Although the spreading of television has resulted in a rapid fall in the number of the cinema-going public (75 million in 1971, as against 140 million spectators in 1960), film production shows a lively development, partly explained—paradoxically enough—by an influence of television. In 1971, 143 features films were manufactured (including features prepared with electronic recording for television), 374 news, documentaries and shorts were prepared, while the number of dubbed films was 375.

Although record production is on what might be termed as the outskirts of the mass communication system, it is still worth our attention that the circulation of LPs has more than doubled in a period of ten years, and, within that, the average of classical musical recordings shows a tendency to increase. This positive trend has certainly been promoted by the fact that, as against most countries in the world, stereo records (more than one-third of the total output in 1971) are sold at the same price as mono records.

In 1972, 7,293 books were published in Hungary, in a total number of 70 million copies. The figures reflect a dynamic development: in the past seven years, the number of new titles increased by 60 per cent and that of copies by 30 per cent. In 1972, every seventh work and every third copy was a book of literary value for adults or young people. In the past few years, copies in the field of novels and short stories have shown a faster increase than any other branch of literature, and the increasing interest in volumes of poetry deserves special attention: in 1972, the average number of copies in which volumes of poetry were published was 9,000. Fifty-two per cent of all volumes of literature published in 1972 were by Hungarian authors, 48 per cent were works by foreign writers. The output of scientific, popularizing and technical books has doubled in comparison to the figure of 1965, while the average number of copies increased by 34 per cent.

4 National communication policies

The system of mass communication carries out its activity within the institutional framework of a given society. Therefore—beyond social automatism—it is subjected not only to principles or norms relating directly to press, information or cultural policies: other facets of social practice may also sometimes implicitly have an effect on mass communication activity.

The political principle, for instance, according to which in a socialist society—thus also in Hungary—culture is not a commodity, i.e. cultural supply should not be determined by market mechanisms, means—as will be seen later—that questions of commercial viability basically do not influence the principles governing the structure and operation of the Hungarian mass communication system.

At other times the stand taken by national bodies on issues in other fields of social activity may indirectly influence information policies.

According to the guiding principles of the science policy elaborated by the Hungarian Socialist Worker's Party in 1969

every researcher has the right to discuss the principles and results of this work in a scientific forum. In making use of research results responsible decisions should be taken as to which of the problems may be referred to political bodies, which should be published in scholarly journals or books and which of them are ripe for the widest publicity [15].

In some cases, the principles of communication policy are expressed explicitly and take the legal form of provisions, political declarations, economic regulations and plans affecting the entire system of mass communication or some of its subsystems. The mode of expression, sphere of activity and validity may differ, but all include some of the common basic principles rooted in the value and norm system of Hungarian society.

Mass communication in Hungary is a means for the realization of the worker' rule. As a means of political power it transmits information from the government and other central organs of the society to the masses and from the masses back to these centres of decision; it shapes the people's *Weltanschauung* (philosophy of life) and mobilizes and organizes for the common tasks of building a new society.

Mass communication has an active role in the shaping of the new type of personality: that of the socialist man. For this purpose it offers the public exact, quick and critical information covering—to quote Lenin—'every aspect of reality'; it tries to reflect real structures and relations in the world differentiating between 'incidental', unessential and 'organic', essential elements of socio-historical progress; it helps to mobilize audiences and awaken their consciousness; and finally, it tries not to overrate its own role and to look at information as it is: an indispensable element of social action but not a substitute for it[16].

As follows in part from the foregoing, mass communication purposefully and openly evaluates social processes and events. The explicit presence of this value-moment restricts the manipulative potentiality of mass communication[17].

Finally, also, the formal-structural principle can be found almost in every declaration, official stand, provision of law conditioning the activity of the communication system on a national level in that they do not refer only to the system of mass communication but to the whole complex of social channels conveying culture and information[18].

The most comprehensive statement concerning national communication policies is found in the constitution of the Hungarian People's Republic originally adopted by parliament in 1949 and developed and partly modified in 1972. Article 62 of the constitution deals directly with social information:

Conforming to the interests of the socialism of the people, the Hungarian People's Republic ensures for its citizens freedom of speech, freedom of the press, and freedom of assembly.

The Hungarian constitution not only defines the rights of citizens but deals also with the necessary conditions for the exercise of such rights. That is why articles 59–60 describing the right to education and the freedom of scientific and artistic creation, although of a more general validity, can in part be related to processes of social communication, as can article 61, paragraph 3, ensuring the legal basis for nationals of others countries living in Hungary to avail themselves of all forms of communication—including mass communication—in their mother tongue.

Article 59, paragraph 1: The Hungarian People's Republic ensures the right to education for every citizen. Paragraph 2: The Hungarian People's Republic implements this right by extending public education and making it general, by means of free and obligatory primary, secondary and higher education, extension courses for adults, and financial support for those receiving education.

Article 60: The Hungarian People's Republic guarantees the freedom of scientific and artistic creative activity.

Article 61, paragraph 3: The Hungarian People's Republic guarantees equality of rights to all nationalities living in its territory, the use of their mother tongue, education in their mother tongue, preservation and cultivation of their own culture.

Other legal regulations of mass communication can be in decrees and in articles of the criminal and civil codes.

The most general regulation covering mass communication problems is decree 26/1959/V.1./Gov. It provides almost a uniform framework for all the regulations passed since the liberation of Hungary, at the same time setting aside outdated press regulations enacted before the Second World War. The decree deals with the problems of licence to publish papers and periodicals, with the legal problems of distribution as well as with the procedure of qualifying statement which—according to the introduction of the decree—'efficiently ensures legality and protects the rightful interests of the citizens'.

Two important paragraphs of the section on qualifying statement:

Article 13, paragraph 1: The administrative, economic or social body or organization about which, or the person concerning whom, a periodical or a radio or television transmission has disseminated or published an untrue fact, or distorted true facts, may demand a qualifying statement to be published by the said periodical, or by the Hungarian Radio and Television, within thirty days following the date of publication or transmission. If the untrue publication violates the public interest, the competent minister (or head of any organ of national authority) may demand publication of the correction.

Article 15, paragraph 1: Should a periodical, radio or television fail to publish the correction, the party demanding the correction may place a claim with the responsible editor of the periodical, with the president of the Hungarian Radio and Television, or—in the case of local broadcasts—with the head of the local studio.

In the system of Hungarian mass communication there is no censorship. The editors-in-chief and the president of the Hungarian Radio and Television, acting as representatives of the owners—that is the people—have full responsibility over the management and editorial policies of the given medium and are responsible for everything published in the paper or broadcast on radio and television—as shown also by the procedure of qualifying statement.

The Criminal Code (act V/1964) declares that incitement, warmongering, dissemination of rumours, defamation, libel and offence against the dead or their memory shall be deemed offences if committed by the press or other reproduction processes. The Civil Code (act IV/1959) also contains some references to the citizen–mass communication relationship, with a definite stress on the legal protection of the individual.

Article 81, paragraph 2: Shall be deemed to be violations of the rights pertaining to the person of the citizen, in particular: all detrimental discrimination of any kind because of sex, nationality or religion, violation of the liberty of conscience of the citizens, restriction of personal freedom, and bodily injury to, or defamation of, the citizen.

Article 82, paragraph 2: The protection of rights pertaining to persons in their capacity as such includes in like manner the protection of good reputation.

Article 83, paragraph 2: The misuse of the likeness or the recorded voice of another person, particularly the unauthorized utilization, reproduction, publication and alteration of such image or record shall constitute a violation of the rights pertaining to persons in their capacity as such.

Article 85, paragraph 1: A person who has been offended in any of his rights pertaining to his person in his capacity as such may, according to the special circumstances of the case, make the following claims under the civil law:

(a) he may ask the Court to state and declare the commission of the wrong;
(b) he may require the wrong to be discontinued and the tort-feasor to be enjoined from doing further wrong;
(c) he may claim that the tort-feasor give satisfaction either by declaration or in some other appropriate manner, and that due publicity be given, if need be, by the tort-feasor, or at his expense, to the satisfaction given by the tort-feasor to him;
(d) he may claim that the injurious situation be brought to an end, that the state prior to the commission of the wrong be restored by the tort-feasor, or at his expense, further, that the thing produced by the wrong be destroyed or deprived of its wrongful character.

Paragraph 2: Should the violation of any right pertaining to persons in their capacity as such have resulted in damage to property, then compensation for damages shall be due, too, according to the rules of responsibility under the civil law.

The above forms of legal regulation of mass communication processes, expressed for the most part in prohibitions or in the sanctions against offences to citizens or social institutions, are to be found in the legal system of practically every state—naturally on different levels of implementation.

The regulation of the Hungarian mass communication system includes, however, legal forms which go beyond these principles as formulated originally during the period of liberal democracy of the last century. They appear not so much in the form of prohibitions but rather as a stimulation of one or another form of communication and they generally refer to the historically new aspects of the relationship of society and mass communication.

It has been mentioned, for example, that a specific characteristic of mass communication in Hungary is the mobilizing and organizing function of press, radio and television. Mass communication, however, has the power of mobilization only if the citizens are convinced that their initiatives and propositions find their way towards realization or that, at least, competent authorities go into the merits of these suggestions. This is promoted by a governmental decree, the first three paragraphs of which deserve full quotation here as they reflect not only a specific aspect of mass communication mechanisms but also illustrate the possibilities of the positive, incentive type of regulation.

1. If any periodical (daily, weekly), the Hungarian Radio and Television, the Hungarian News Agency (hereinafter the press) has published a proposition or criticism, submits the text and asks for an answer within five days after publication, the direct supervisory authority of the state organ concerned (the head of its direct controlling organ) is required to examine the proposition or criticism and give the editor an answer. The answer should be sent to the editor within thirty days after the delivery of the publication and it should contain the findings of the examination as well as the measures taken.

2. If the administrative body approached is not authorized to give the answer, it should advise the editor of this fact within five days after having taken delivery of the publication and should forward the claim to the authorized administrative body.

3. If, in spite of having been approached, the administrative body does not meet its obligation within the given deadline, upon the report of the editor, the direct supervisory body and the competent minister (head of an organization of national authority) is obliged to proceed in the matter without delay to give an answer and, depending on the circumstances, he may call the person in default to account.

Provisions of law—even if they are of a positive, stimulating character—serve only as a framework for the operation of mass communication. Decisions, resolutions and official stands conforming, to a greater or lesser extent to national communication policies, come into being within this framework and exercise their influence thereby.

The principles of information—viewed from the aspect of content— were laid down most recently in the 'Communication Decree', embodying the position taken by the Political Committee of the Hungarian Socialist Workers' Party on 8 June 1965. The decree analyses the interrelations between information, public opinion, and the development of socialist democracy from several points of view. Among others the decree states that

openness, sincerity and completeness of information are indispensable elements of democracy, necessary conditions for the shaping of socialist consciousness, the active public life of the masses as well as the establishment of trust between the Party and the masses.

Attitudes on fundamental principles of social communication are often developed at official gatherings, where politicians, state executives and operators of mass communication meet. The latest important meeting of this kind was the National Reunion of Journalists in December 1971, where János Kádár, First Secretary of the Central Committee of the Hungarian Socialist Workers' Party took the floor.

After analysing several theoretical and practical questions relating to communication policies, János Kádár spoke of socialist mass communication as a specific two-way information channel system and stressed that this should be reflected also in the selection of topics:

... if the masses do not deal with the problems of leadership to the necessary extent something must be done about it: questions on the agenda of the leaders must be publicised. If, however, the leaders do not pay the necessary attention to what the masses are thinking, then the leaders must be helped and obliged to overcome these problems [19].

In the past few years information and mass communication have been more and more often discussed whether within the families, at party congresses, during coffee-breaks or in scholarly debates in the Academy of Sciences. The technical reason is that thanks to the rapid development of television, political programmes come to the audience's attention to an extent[20] that, in the past, was feasible only with entertainment programmes. Another deeper, historico-political reason is that a strong consensus has been developed in Hungarian society as regards the following: for the advancement of new, socialist-type forms of action in democracy, for the dynamic development of the institutional system so that it may be adapted to these forms an ever more up-to-date process of social information is needed reflecting already the values and norms of future society.

In the ideological and political orientation of mass communication the Hungarian Socialist Workers' Party plays the most prominent part. Far from being a formal hierarchical contact, this orientation is rather a kind of co-operation where autonomous units of the mass communication system and various organs and bodies of the party meet in order to elaborate common strategies towards the common goals: those of the socialist society. Thus, this process of orientation takes on varied and rather flexible forms, though all of them have some common traits: they deal with matters of principle rather than with details of media practice; they refer rather to policy dimensions of media operation than to managerial dimensions; they orientate by information rather than by interpreting information; they promote active participation of all media people in the political life.

During the last few years social research has also been contributing to this dialogue between the party and mass communication. After the tenth Party Congress, for instance, early in 1970, the Agitation and Propaganda Committee of the party and the Presidency of the Hungarian Academy of Sciences recommended a list of social issues to be studied by universities and research institutes. The research has now been going on for three years and the findings will be built into the working documents of the eleventh congress of the party. Each of these issues under study closely relates to current problems of Hungarian society and two of them bear direct relation to the communication system: one examines the various aspects of political communication, the other is concerned with the culture-transmitting and entertaining functions of mass communication.

The following are the most important organs for the practical implementation of guiding principles in the system of mass communication: as regards the State administration, the Information Bureau of the Council of Ministers; for the socio-professional aspects, the Association of Hungarian Journalists; and in other respects those social bodies which act as direct supervisory authorities over editorial boards.

The Information Bureau is an organ of national authority exercising supervision over the operation of the mass communication system. Besides organizing information and propaganda relating to the work of the supreme legislative and administrative bodies, it participates in the preparation of all legal provisions regarding mass communication, grants licences, distributes the paper contingent at the disposal of the press, takes part in policy decisions relating to financial, labour, wage and price problems in the domain of mass communication, and prepares the development plans for the system of mass communication.

The Association of Hungarian Journalists as a professional association will be discussed in some detail later. We mention here only that its operations are not restricted to professional and welfare tasks but it is also in charge of the education of the generation of journalists, the further training of mid-career newsmen and the organization of the means of keeping them informed. Through these activities the association is an integral part of the management of the mass communication system.

No private person may start a paper or radio or television broadcast in Hungary. Newspapers are published by various political and social bodies. Among the national dailies, for instance, *Népszabadság* is the paper of the Hungarian Socialist Workers' Party, *Népszava* that of the trade unions and *Magyar Nemzet* is under the sponsorship of the People's Patriotic Front. These organizations through their own governing bodies control and guide the work of their papers and supervise it also from the point of view of conformity with the given aims and endeavours of the organization concerned.

Although the role of economic regulators in the implementation of communication policies is of secondary importance compared to the politico-ideological means of orientation or to the levers embodied in administrative mechanisms, they deserve mention.

Mass communication institutions in Hungary are either publicly financed institutions, or economic units operating as enterprises. Their economic systems, their interests differ according to type, consequently the possibilities of influencing them by economic means towards the goals of national communication policies also differ.

The most important among the publicly financed institutions is the Hungarian Radio and Television. Both its income and expenses are planned in the yearly State budgets and so must be approved by parliament. Income originating predominantly in subscriptions[21] covers operation costs, the sum to be paid to the Hungarian Post for the maintenance and operation of the network of transmitters, leaving a considerable amount for the financial support of other institutions in the cultural and educational subsystems through the channels of the national budget. This means that the modern, electronic media of communication give indirectly important material support to the traditional means of disseminating knowledge and culture, from museums to theatres.

The Hungarian Radio and Television, being a publicly financed institution, is not directly interested in increasing its income. Nevertheless, since the reform of economic management in 1968, publicly financed institutions also have had the right to found economic enterprises. Grasping this opportunity, the Hungarian Radio and Television created a Commercial Bureau engaged in advertisement[22], acting as a publisher of books, selling magnetic tapes and dealing with minor business transactions. The net income of this activity is left for the most part with the Hungarian Radio and Television and is

31

devoted to welfare purposes (resthouses, nurseries, material assistance for staff housing projects).

The other basic form of economy among mass media institutions is the enterprise. A wide segment of mass communication works in this form: the printed press. Nevertheless, it would be a mistake to think of individual newspapers and journals as 'profit-seeking' economic units. It is the publishing house—handling several kinds of publications: newspapers, journals, sometimes books as well—which has the legal and economic attributes of an enterprise, while the editorial boards of individual papers, in effect, work along the principles of publicly financed institutions. They have no direct material interest in raising the circulation of their own paper, but only indirectly, through the publisher's activity as a whole. In this specific construction the publisher plays the role of a 'buffer' which absorbs possible economic shocks and enables the editorial boards to work free of market considerations, directing their full energy towards the realization of the principles of cultural and communication policies.

Up to the economic reform of 1968, practical operation of the two types of mass media organizations did not greatly differ. Since prices were not based on production costs but were fixed by central authorities reflecting the innate logic of an overcentralized planning, the economy of enterprises had much in common with that of publicly financed institutions. As a result of the economic reform this situation underwent a gradual transformation. Prices began to approach the costs of real inputs: printing costs were raised by 26 per cent, paper by 28 per cent, distribution by 71 per cent from 1967 to 1968. In the case of the daily paper *Népszava,* for instance, modifications in the price structure resulted in an increase of production costs from 46 to 71 fillers per copy. Thus, in 1971 every copy of this paper showed a loss of 3.8 fillers, leaving advertising income out of consideration[23]. This forced the press to meet the growing demands of the economy for advertising. But, so as not to endanger the basic political and cultural functions of mass communication, the proportion of advertisement in the total space of the papers was not to surpass the rate reached in 1970.

Part of the publishers' profit is redirected to the central resources of national development, a certain share is distributed among the staff of the papers and the publishing houses, and finally, a not negligible share is reinvested in technological development of the publishing house, supplementing central resources for investment. This process of technological development is really needed: up to the middle sixties the technical infrastructure of the printed press was rather obsolete and a dynamic development has taken place only in the past few years.

Some cultural institutions, classed sometimes as part of the system of mass communication, also work as enterprises, such as record companies and the film manufacturers. They have a direct interest in increasing their income, for higher income means higher profits, a part of which they can distribute among their employees in the form bonuses and awards. Although for this reason they are definitely 'market-oriented', here, too, side by side with other regulators, specific economic stimulators enforce the principles of national communication policies.

Built into the planning system of the national economy, their economic plans follow the preferences of the society as a whole.

With regard to their message and artistic standard, the films produced are classified by a jury consisting of experts and critics. Fully independent of the marketing possibilities of the films, this classification influences to a great extent the amount of premiums those involved in production will receive.

After each product of a lower cultural, but predictably higher marketing value is issued in the field of book publication, film and record production as well as in the field of applied and fine arts, the producing and distributing companies must pay a definite fee to a central cultural fund. The amounts gained from this 'kitsch-tax' can then be channelled for the financing of works that are more desirable from the viewpoint of both cultural and communications policies.

The methodology of economic, or in a wider sense social, planning in Hungary distinguishes between medium- and long-term plans. Short-term plans cover 1-2 years, medium-term plans are the Five-Year Plans and long-term plans relate to 10-15 years or even longer periods.

These three levels of planning are to be found also in the mass communication system. Short-term plans are usually programmes of activity or campaign plans, elaborated for the most part at the level of the editorial boards[24] outlining the goals and tasks of the mass communication in respect of important social events or processes. Medium- and long-term plans aim at the development of individual media or of the entire system of mass communication. These plans are generally prepared by national policy-making bodies and are organically linked to the over-all process of social planning in Hungary.

The fourth Five-Year Plan (1971–75) includes, for instance, the five-year plan of newspaper publishing. Based on the principles of the national communication policies, taking into consideration the probable changes in the living standards of the population, the demands of the reading public, the planned technological development of the press and the possibilities of distribution, it indicates the directions of press-development for this period. It stresses among others that development in this field should not mean primarily starting new papers, but increasing the circulation of those already existing, the improvement of the technical-aesthetic standard of layout, and the perfecting of the message itself. Moreover, in this intensive type of development, mass circulation papers should have priority over publications of narrower scope.

An essential feature of the economic reform begun in the late sixties was the raising of the scientific standards and the improvement of the efficiency of the system of planning. This tendency found expression in the growing importance of long-range plans within the system of planning, and in fact that planning of strictly economic processes was gradually supplemented by forecasts and plans relating to social processes of a non-directly economic character which, nevertheless, have an impact on the economic domain.

This type of development of social planning makes it possible and even necessary that the most important long-range goals and the ways and means of development be formulated with respect to the communication system as well. These long-range plans of the mass communication media may be either plans comprising the most significant aspects of long-term development of a given medium, or plans of a more complex nature where the prospects of mass communication constitute only some aspects of the whole field planned. Hungarian planning practice has offered examples of both types in the past few years.

In 1969, the Hungarian Radio elaborated its development plan for the seventies[25]. In this plan the long-range conceptions of programming policy and programme development are based on forecasts of the national development in the next fifteen years. It naturally outlines also the most important parameters of development as regards the staff and the technological infrastructure to meet the demands of the over-all development of broadcasting.

Within the framework of long-range social planning the development plan of cultural activity was also prepared in 1972[26]. This first plan in Hungary dealing primarily with the intellectual social sphere and the institutional system embodying and serving it, though in rather general outline, drafts the prospects of all culture transmitting institutions, including those of the mass media.

These plans, far from containing detailed instructions or directives of a strictly obligatory character, make up a system of guiding principles and preferences expressing the specific teleological way of thinking and behaviour of the socialist society. They provide a firm ground for the realization of national communication policies under political, legal and economic regulations as flexible and dynamic as possible. They also permit the formulation of medium-level communication policies and plans by the editorial bodies.

5 Policies of the mass media

In the press, the policies of editorial offices are usually not set down in writing. In view of the number of journalists employed, editorial offices are relatively small intellectual workshops in which the individual's social-emotional ambitions would be unachievable, even temporarily, unless he strove to conform to norms dictated by the accepted target system, daily manifesting itself, if only tacitly. In these editorial offices it has never become necessary to have statutes worked out and accepted. Formal and informal relations are not so differentiated as in other official organizations; as against coolness and reserve the full devotion of the individual is sought. In such an atmosphere the editorial office's policies do not appear to be dictated from the outside by the organization but, in most cases, they can hardly be distinguished from the individual's ambitions.

The basic fact of Hungarian society is the socialist system, and it follows that editorial offices constitute an integral part of the political target system. Consequently, the most important role in forming the editorial office's policies will be played by the national communication policies worked out in political workshops, with constant reference to the experience of the editorial offices and the opinions of the journalists.

On the other hand, more and more workshops take part in the working out of the national communication policies since, obviously, it is impossible to separate artificially the task of marking politico-economic decisions from that of motivating and explaining them. Moreover, it cannot be ignored that economical-technical knowledge and possibilities cannot always be reflected clearly in the decisions because possibly irrational yet influential public opinion on certain questions must be taken into account. Therefore it is through continuous co-operation and frequent consultation and discussion among journalists and specialists in mass communication that directives at the national level applicable to actual situations are arrived at. These must fit functionally into general policy and also be capable of being broken down into policies for editorial offices.

Editorial policies reflect traditions of the offices as well as the social parameters and the special requirements of the readers. These traditional features are very important indeed; not infrequently the reading of a particular journal has run in a family for generations, indicating a family habit, and often also the family's position in the social structure[27].

For generations workers had been reading *Népszava* (The People's

Voice) for example, the oldest Hungarian daily, which was the only legal workers' journal before the Second World War. A similar role was played by *Magyar Nemzet* (Hungarian Nation) for 'humanist' intellectuals; its programme based on the idea of popular-national unity and intellectual tone impressed most teachers, artists, doctors and civil servants.

Traditions such as this and similar ones have brought about the organic division of labour in the press, but the same historical development resulted also in traditions sometimes giving way to modern requirements, e.g. nearly all daily papers now try to fill the gap created by the sudden restructuring of the intellectuals when the tremendous need for scientific technical specialists brought into being almost immediately a social group whose interest differed essentially from that of intellectuals in the traditional sense. The most recent experience generally encourages heads of editorial offices to give a more definite character to the journals and—preserving the basic, essential features of the model already formed—to take into account, with increased attention, the social parameters and particular requirements of their readership[28].

Hungarian Radio and Television works with a huge apparatus as compared with the editorial offices of the various journals. Therefore, in many respects its management cannot dispense with the customary well-tried means used in big organizations. Thus also, their principles of programme policy, for example, are sometimes set down in written documents, thus lending support to the basic aims of management without restricting creativity, individual initiative and the relative, yet indispensable, autonomy of radio and television workshops.

It is among the postulates of the artistic programme policies of the Hungarian Radio and Television—reflecting the principles of national cultural policies—that socialist values be supported; that works ideologically slightly ambiguous but not anti-socialist be tolerated; that all anti-socialist tendencies denying basic moral standards, and opening the door to corruption of taste and decadence be forbidden. In regard to popular education the Hungarian Radio and Television allots a prominent role to the propagation of Marxist-Leninist ideology, at the same time making it very clear that the advancement of political knowledge cannot be considered an exclusive task, just as the notion of popular education cannot be limited to literature, music, or fine arts. All this notwithstanding electronic communication can establish a certain order of preference in its popular educational programmes; it can respond to the requirements of the current conditions, events and interests of society. Thus, in the last decade attention turned mainly to human sciences: psychology, sociology, anthropology, urbanism. Under such circumstances, electronic communication gives preference to these topics as opposed to say, literature of the Middle Ages, without contesting the value of the latter in the universality of culture.

The management of the Hungarian Radio and Television usually sets down in writing those aspects of important political events that affect their programme policy.

The last such document contained conclusions regarding programme policy, drawn from the tenth congress of the Hungarian Socialist Workers' Party. The congress was one of social consolidation, it did not mark any sudden turns, but approved and confirmed the policies, developments and aims of past years. Hence the slogan adopted by the tenth congress: the task is now to continue the building of socialism at an improved level. The relevant document of the Hungarian Radio and Television is clearly concerned, then, with the task of better programme-making, development of the creative atmosphere, moral and financial improvement, and constructive programme criticism. In regard to contents the document states that priority is to be given to realistic representation of the life and concerns of working-class people; proving the interdependence of workers and peasants; the further strengthening of confidence in the party, its politics, and the social system; the development of socialist democracy in all spheres of social life, drawing a finer material and moral distinction between excellent, average and poor accomplishments.

Some years after the Second World War personal incomes levelled up within certain limits—with a relatively low national income per head. Thus the principle of socialist distribution according to which everyone works according to his abilities and receives remuneration according to his work could not be put to effect. This egalitarianism had its political advantages undoubtedly in a period in which material goods were scarce and had to be allocated to meet prevailing needs. Later, however, when the socialist economy had already become stronger, to maintain egalitarianism would have created an obstacle to development, because it offered no inducement for individual achievement. It has become more and more obvious that the path to the society of equality leads through inequalities in certain periods of building socialism, but that socialism has always preserved the basic principle distinguishing it from capitalism: the power of the working class, the public ownership of the means of production, the basic situation in which it is impossible for one man to exploit the other, and at the same time differentiation between personal incomes but in such a way that family incomes should not show too great variations. The new system of economic management has aimed from the beginning to arouse the interest of members of society in efficient work, within the framework of a planned economy, in order to assure better results than were achieved during the earlier periods of socialist distribution[29].

Under these circumstances journalists had not only to use mass communication channels to explain reforms, but also, in their own living conditions, changes were taking place encouraging them to concentrate more on the results of their work.

Earlier only 5 per cent of the staff member's salary could be awarded by the editor as a bonus for extraordinary performance. Given that journalists' fees were not very high, this amount could not be effective in initiating real effort. It had rather a moral importance as an expression of appreciation for outstanding performance and special effort. By the end of the sixties conditions were ripe for application of the principle of socialist distribution, namely that everybody should work to his abilities and share the goods on the basis of work performed. Further impetus was given to development, the development of mass media included. The pace of work was accelerated in the editorial offices and ability, quick work and alertness increased, although not to the detriment of authenticity. The introduction of the new system of economic management revealed that the system of salaries and bonuses is part and parcel of editorial policy.

In the course of the first three years of the economic reform the degree of inner integration within editorial offices increased considerably as a result of material incentives, organizational discipline improved, and real capabilities were better exhibited. Newspapers of better quality were published, and more professional journalists were employed in editorial offices. However, as compared to the relatively low journalists' salaries, the amounts to be allotted to incentive bonuses in addition to salaries, if the desired aim was really to be achieved, were too large. Thus, at certain national daily papers the bonuses distributed monthly appeared to be almost an adjustment of salaries, and caused such fluctuations in incomes that there was a feeling of uncertainty and defencelessness among the journalists, the bonuses became sources of constant unrest, and sometimes pushed into the background the solution of political tasks. This new contradiction could only be satisfactorily settled by raising the journalists' salaries, establishing a normal relation between nominal salaries and monthly bonuses. This last measure was taken in 1971 when the president of the Government Information Bureau, in agreement with the Ministry of Finance, Ministry of Labour and the Hungarian Printing, Paper and Press Workers' Union, agreed to the financial conditions necessary for putting the measure into effect[30].

In the sphere of mass communication the incentive resulting from economic reform was evidenced mainly in a quicker recruitment of talent, in the development of attitudes which are oriented more to results, and in better and more disciplined work.

38

6 Relations between mass communication and its public

An actor 'co-operates' with his audience in all performances, he is conscious of its presence, and of his success or failure. The journalist's position is different: he knows that his printed thoughts will be read, or that his voice is listened to on the radio, or that his smallest gesture is watched on television, but he is not in a position to experience reactions directly because he is not present at the places reached by his messages through the mass media. The only way to make this contact is to link mass media closely with the public, and of course, in this process the journalist's personal advantage should not be of primary importance.

There are institutional guarantees for building such a relation, made possible because the 'owners' of mass communication media are generally social organizations such as the Hungarian Socialist Workers' Party, the trade union movement, the Patriotic People's Front movement, the youth association, local communist party organizations, professional associations, etc. These social organizations include the whole of the nation, and when the bodies, elected democratically, represent the 'owners' interest in the media over which they have direct control, they also have an indirect control over mass communication in the name of the masses, they state opinions in the name of their respective organizations, give advice and state requirements.

Among social organizations, the Hungarian Socialist Workers' Party is of course not just one among the others. As the leading political force of Hungarian society it also has a determining influence, through its members, on the activities of organs over which it has no direct control. This influence, however, does not manifest itself in the management of affairs, but in the issuing of directives governing national communication policies, as these stand above particular interest.

A most important element in the relation between mass communication and the public is of course, the journalist himself. His profession makes it indispensable that he constantly meet members of the public, and this contact has a direct effect on his view of society, his thinking, and his judgements. Nor can it be considered of secondary importance that journalists in this country have already become familiar with the lives of working people in their parents' home, that they gain their first basic experience among people who labour to produce material and spiritual goods. This is clearly borne out in Table 3 which gives a classification of journalists according to social origin[31].

TABLE 3

| Journalist's age | Father's profession | | | | | |
| | Professional and white collar | | Occupations of physical work | | | |
	Total	Professional	Total	Skilled and semi-skilled workers	Unskilled workers	Peasants
Under 29	64	27	36	31	4	1
Between 30 and 39	47	15	53	37	6	10
Between 40 and 49	36	14	64	42	7	15
Over 50	58	20	42	31	3	8

A form of relation with the public found in the Leninist tradition is known in the history of the press as 'workers' correspondence'. Lenin attributed enormous importance to the workers being heard not only through their representatives but also directly on all sorts of questions. He did not think it was sufficient to do everything in the workers' interest: he emphasized that workers' activities were essential in the whole of economic, political and intellectual life[32]. He saw a manifestation of this principle when workers and peasants—people not used to writing—sent letters to the editors of journals telling about their attitudes to society, their concerns, the difficulties facing them, the results achieved, instances of corruption on a small or large scale, in a word, about everything that occupied them.

The creation of other forums of public life, the multichannel information flow, the improvement of media changed the original function of the workers' correspondents to some extent, but it is not only in deference to tradition that this initiative of early origin has not been abandoned. The citizen who writes letters to the editorial office still considers the latter a forum of direct democracy, and usually is convinced that he may help, with his remarks, to correct the errors and bureaucratic excesses of the administrative, commercial and cultural apparatus. This conviction is not false, as correspondence departments of editorial offices are obliged not only to answer all letters indicating the name and address of sender, but also to give concrete advice on the most varied questions, to publicize some of the problems of public interest, and in the case of affairs and complaints of minor importance, to start or to suggest investigation with the aid of the responsible authorities. An average of two thousand letters are delivered monthly to the journal *Népszabadság* (People's Freedom), organ of the central committee of the party, and five thousand letters are received monthly by the correspondence department of the Hungarian Radio and Television.

Readers' conferences are also an old Leninist tradition, in the course of which the members on the staff of editorial offices meet, from time to time, the representatives of various strata of society—readers, viewers, listeners —and discuss with them their editorial policies, their ideas, speak about their troubles, hear various opinions, criticism, suggestions.

The research work carried out by the research units of Hungarian Radio and Television, and various publishing houses is also in the interest of relations with the public.

Previously the Mass Communication Research Centre of Hungarian Radio and Television studied the size of the radio and television audience, its satisfaction with programmes, listening or viewing habits. They also carried out public opinion research regularly, and tried to analyse the sociological, socio-psychological and methodological characteristics of the process of mass communication. The centre's tasks have increased recently as they more regularly investigate questions concerned with the whole system of social communication. This has become inevitable because the understanding of the mass communication system, and a complex exploration of its possibilities, does not allow the exclusion of any factor from the research work.

An important element in research concerned with the public is the feedback of information about the public—in the form of programmes and articles—to the public. This is an indication of the frankness of relations with the public in socialist mass communication, and evidence of its desire to seem neither more nor less than it is in reality.

7 Relations between mass communication and information sources

For authentic and quick mass communication the first requirement is that mass communication media themselves should have quick and authentic information. Special importance is therefore attached to informing editorial offices in due time about current problems, home and foreign events, tasks to be fulfilled and decisions that may be of public interest. This is accomplished, in particular, by the system of press conferences which may take various forms.

Regular press conferences, held by political institutions concerning editors-in-chief to orient the most important questions.

Head of various special agencies, ministries, superior authorities, hold press conferences to which the specialists of the editorial offices are usually invited.

Heads of various special agencies, ministries, superior authorities, hold press conferences upon their own decision and usually invite journalists with whom they have previously established fruitful co-operation.

An essential point that holds true for every kind of information is that it is left to the editors to make use of the information given, in the form they consider best.

The Hungarian News Agency, a semi-offical government news service provides indispensable information to the mass communication media[33]. This institution was founded by two stenographers, Hugó Maszák and Géza Egyes, in 1880. In addition to supplying official publications, the main objective at present is to provide the Hungarian press, radio and television with foreign and home news, and also other customers at home and abroad.

The Hungarian News Agency has 1,036 employees, among whom there are 180 journalists and 44 press photographers. Telex messages amount to a daily average of 30,000 words. The service receives regularly material supplied by AP (New York), UPI (New York), AFP (Paris), Reuter (London), DPA (Hamburg), Tass (Moscow), ADN (Berlin), PAP (Warsaw), CTK (Prague), Agerpress (Bucharest), BTA (Sofia), ATA (Tirana), New China (Peking), Tanyug (Belgrade), MENA (Cairo), VNA (Hanoi), Kyodo (Tokyo), APS (Algiers) and SANA (Damascus). From time to time it also uses material supplied by APA (Vienna), Prensa Latina (Havana), KCNA (Pyongyang), IPS (Montevideo), Anatolie Turkey (Ankara), JPS (Tokyo), Moncame (Ulan Bator), Tunis Afrique Presse (Tunis), Indinfo (New Delhi), MAP (Rabat), ANSA (Rome), Fineuro (European Economic Service), INA (Tel Aviv).

The Hungarian News Agency has its own correspondents in Moscow, Berlin, Warsaw, Prague, Bucharest, Sofia, Belgrade, Vienna, Bonn, London, Paris, Washington, Cairo, Peking, Hanoi and Rome. Out of the 140 to 160 pages of foreign political news supplied to editorial offices, 100 to 110 pages are translations of material received from foreign agencies and 40 to 50 pages cover information from Hungarian correspondents. The agency sends special correspondents 150–180 times yearly to report important international events.

Information from news agencies and Hungarian correspondents is completed by a radio monitoring service. The Hungarian News Agency informs its customers about events abroad and at home by a rapid photograph service, supplying an average of 2,000 photographs monthly to the Hungarian newspapers and television. In addition, the editorial office of the foreign news services 400 dailies and periodicals; they publish a bilingual daily *Daily News—Neueste Nachrichten,* and 22 bulletins among which the most important are the following: *News of Metallurgy and Machine Industry* (Kohászati és Gépipari Információk), *Commerce* (Kereskedelem), *Agriculture in the World* (A világ mezőgazdasága), *Modern Management* (Korszerü vezetés), *Law Information* (Jogi tudósitó), *Articles on Economy from the International Press* (Gazdasági cikkek a nemzetközi sajtóból), *Theoretical Articles* (Elméleti cikkek).

In creating and guaranteeing relations between the various information sources and mass media an important role is played by the Information Bureau of the Council of Ministers, a government organ exercising control over press activities.

The Information Bureau is supervised by the government through the President of the Cabinet; the president and vice-president of the bureau are appointed by the government. The president of the bureau acts as spokesman for the government. The bureau organizes the supply of information on the activities of the highest executive and administrative bodies of the State. It also assures freedom of press coverage of important national and international events. At the same time it is responsible—without prejudice to its information duties—for the protection of State and official secrets, and military secrets concerned with defence.

The press departments of ministries are also among the institutional beneficiaries of relations between mass communication and sources of information[34]. The information sources for the ministries are especially important in view of the fact that these institutions perform tasks of organization and direction in all spheres of the national economy, and in most social spheres.

The press departments of ministries are responsible for seeing to it that all important information in their own field reaches the public through the channels of mass communication. They must be prepared any time to give all possible help to journalists which they may request (e.g. preparation of interviews; gathering of data and statistics; collection of material for reports; consultations with specialists, etc.).

In a certain sense, the information relations between the mass communication media and the enterprises were modified by the reform of economic management. Of course, even prior to reform, the publishing of local reports and evaluations on the production of material goods, the labour situation and the national economy had played a fundamental role in the activities of mass communication. The so-called production 'propaganda', the extension of the work of the press to cover participation in the organization of the economy are characteristic features of socialist mass communication, since they are essential elements in the Leninist model of the press[35].

The developments after 1968 did not weaken but rather strengthened this principle: a number of obstacles facing the media were removed because the enterprises began to appreciate the value of press publicity in building up their 'image'. Under the new conditions journalists became 'more important' for the managers and are receiving more support in their activity. Economic units are naturally not indifferent to what information the press is spreading about them, since different evaluation can either improve or harm their prestige with consumers and other enterprises, and directly affect their profitability. Apart from the obvious advantages, this situation also carries the danger that the mass communication media may make hidden publicity, or prejudice the credit of the enterprises in the name of production propaganda. Therefore, the practice followed in socialist press-law and press ethics is to take very energetic measures in the event of press actions injurious to social interests.

8 Interrelation of mass media

The co-ordinated activities of the Hungarian mass communication media are based on homogeneous national communication policies and on public ownership.

The editors-in-chief of journals and the president of the Hungarian Radio and Television are personally responsible for the implementation of national communication policies. Co-operation among the media is such that there are no editorial secrets; the heads and their colleagues in the editorial offices are always prepared to co-operate in order to inform the public as quickly and as accurately possible.

They inter-change ideas and plans and make agreements, if necessary, in connexion with certain events, or help each other in other ways. The archives of all editorial offices are available to practically every journalist; correspondents do not hide from each other what they intend to write on foreign and home events; if, for example, the telex machine in one editorial office breaks down, or lines are engaged, another office can be used for taking the messages.

The material of television programmes is often published in the press and questions asked during the political programmes on television are answered and commented on in the press. A good example of this is the highly successful television programme *Fórum*. In this 'question time' programme politicians, economic leaders, foreign political specialists answer in live telecast the questions asked by viewers by telephone. Since, however, this relatively long programme is still not long enough to answer the several hundreds of questions asked, the daily press and one of the political weeklies carry the answers after the programme is finished.

Mass information is a social interest of vital importance, therefore its regulation cannot be entrusted to the market forces—which do exist and in some respects also affect mass communication. Therefore, the various mass media do not consider mutual advertisement of each other's products is a promotion activity.

In a campaign to make the use of radio more general, for example, central and local papers published offers to send the *Radio and Television Times* free for a whole month to buyers of new radio sets, and announced that a 10–15 per cent discount on the prices of the sets would be granted. This applies also in the other direction: the electronic mass media also make a great effort to publicize the activity of the press. When a new central daily newspaper was founded in 1968, the television broadcast several live programmes reporting the aims of the editors, the columns planned, the special line of the journal envisaged, its format, its social-political purposes.

These examples demonstrate that for co-operation among mass communication media public ownership offers an excellent basis; none of the media has any interest in eclipsing or ruining the other.

The large-scale spread of television—as elsewhere in the world—caused a temporary feeling of insecurity among radio and film people. While radio and Hungarian film production became stronger after the temporary shock, television dealt a serious blow to the cinema. The radio quickly found its place in the television world and not only kept but increased its audience, owing mainly to a quick adjustment to the new conditions by adopting new conceptions of programme-making, courageous initiatives—and a modern programme structure. Hungarian film making also made great progress in large part thanks to an increasing number of co-productions by film studios and television.

While in 1960 fifteen feature films and thirteen short films were completed, in 1970 forty-six feature films and one hundred short films were presented. Sixty-six out of the 146 films produced were commissioned for television. At the same time the number of cinemagoers decreased from 140.1 million to 79.6 million.

Local dailies and broadcasting take a special place in the Hungarian system of mass communication. Television, central radio and central dailies are the most appropriate media to bridge major distances between events and recipients, but this function is not to pass on regular information across short distances. As long as the fate of people, their living conditions and possibilities were almost exclusively dependent on central decisions, local information was reduced to minor importance. At that time there was scant interest in the local environment and the restructuring of the use of mass media called for profound social changes. Recently there has taken place a growing decentralization within the economy and the various centres of decision accompanied by the spread of local autonomy. This caused changes in the subscriptions to, and buying of, central and local papers. The readership of local papers has been increasing extremely fast, while some decrease has taken place in the circulation of certain central journals. This change of proportion did not cause any anxiety among the directors of the central journals, since it had been anticipated, in some respects, even planned politically. Indeed it may play a very important part in the development of political activity and the further democratization of public life.

The public ownership of the financial-technical basis has its role in the relations between the various mass media. Within the system of mass communication, the funds must be so distributed that social interest shall prevail over any possible group interests, particular or selfish considerations. Control of the financial-technical basis is the duty of the Information Bureau[36]. The relevant data indicate that, in the distribution of facilities, social demands and priority of political aims are most extensively taken into consideration.

Paper consumption by the press amounted to 21,100 tons in 1960 and 64,500 tons in 1970. The increase of 200 per cent was the result mainly of increased variety and volume, and the sudden greater interest in local newspapers. While in a period of ten years circulation of central daily newspapers hardly changed, that of county and city dailies grew by a yearly average of 50,000. County papers were published in 429,155 copies in 1960, and in 1970 the figure had already reached 780,404.

9 Communication policies and the professional organizations

The Association of Hungarian Journalists was formed in 1945, uniting the journalists who were members of the parties joining the Independent People's Front[37]. The association immediately started organizing help for journalists who were in bad financial straits and it also established the first collective contract for journalists. The association in this way has established a basis for its policy of safeguarding interests.

Parallel with these activities, the association began the expulsion of journalists who were fascists, or opposed to the democratic order, thus greatly assisting the process of political purification of public life under the re-organization.

These steps served as a foundation for the general policy to be followed by the association: the assembling of journalists of progressive and democratic mentality; an active and positive reaction to the trend of development of Hungarian society.

Today the Association of Hungarian Journalists has 3,000 members: 17 per cent under the age of 30, 33 per cent between 30 and 40, 38 per cent between 40 and 50, and 12 per cent over 50 of the total membership. Women account for 22.2 per cent. Within the association there are twenty-seven sections helping to satisfy special interests of the journalists and to find solutions to their special problems. These sections offer a framework for them to express their opinions, state their professional demands and put forward their ideas about mass communication policies. The association has undertaken to assist in the development of press science; it runs the International Journalists' School of Budapest, designates journalists for foreign scholarships, and helps foreign holders of scholarships who come to Hungary. In the course of its activity of safeguarding interests the union proposes measures aiming at improvement of living and working conditions of journalists; it has its own recreation homes open to members on the payment of very small fees; it manages the International Journalists' Recreation House which receives 500 guests every summer from different countries; under the national health service it has its own group of doctors at the disposal of its members; it builds freehold houses and recreation homes at cost prices.

The members of the press belong mostly to the Hungarian Printing, Paper and Press Workers' Union, while most radio and television people belong to the Art Workers' Union. In view of the divided nature of the special organizations and of the fact that the Association of Hungarian Journalists also deals with safeguarding interests of those working in mass communication, the need arose for improving co-ordination of the activities of the organizations involved. Therefore, a co-operation agreement was signed in June 1970, under the terms of which common points of view are to be reached—always after hearing all parties' opinions—on the following important points: assessment of the living and working conditions of journalists and safeguarding their rightful interests in regard to the national health service and recreation; preparation and amendment of legal provisions concerned with mass communication activity; discussions of plans for a general development of the news-service, or for important investments of Hungarian Radio and Television, with special regard to concepts affecting social, cultural and working conditions.

To achieve these aims, the leading bodies of the three organizations concert their plans every six months, and decide at which discussions of the various items on the agenda they want to be represented. In addition, the general secretaries evaluate every six months the experience gained in the course of their co-operation, and also plan the activity of the co-ordination committee set up to carry the agreement into effect[38].

10 System of professional training

Journalists' training schools were introduced in Hungary in 1951. The first experiment was a double one-year course which was completed by a total of 134 students.

After initial experiments, it was in 1953 that in the Arts Faculty of the Eötvös Lórant University a department of journalism was set up with its own professorate offering three-year courses. In addition to general subjects, special subjects included press history, artistic theory and practical learning techniques.

In 1958, the Association of Hungarian Journalists undertook responsibility for the training of journalists in a school-system. In the fifteen years that have since passed, 700 students have completed the Journalists' School, of whom 75 per cent are still members of the profession.

The system of admission was regulated collectively by the Information Bureau and the Association of Hungarian Journalists. The training is postgraduate, so that only in exceptional cases was the Admission and Qualification Committee able to dispense with the required qualification for admission of a university or high school diploma. Candidates are not admitted to the Journalists' School directly upon graduation from the university or high school. At least six months (without university or high-school diploma a minimum of one year) must be spent in practical work in one of the editorial offices, during which time the candidate must obtain the support and recommendation of his chief editor.

The training period is two years, but for persons over 30 years of age it can be reduced to six months. Simultaneously with the pursuit of their studies, students continue to work for the editorial office. Studying is one of their contractual obligations to their employers, and they continue to receive monthly salaries.

In addition to general subjects the programme of the Journalists' School includes: theory of genres, press history, communication theory, correct use of language, style, technical knowledge (page-setting, techniques of radio and television), basic press photography, press ethics and press law, typing and shorthand, writing of special columns.

The School of Dramatic and Cinematic Arts also includes in its programme the training of mass communication specialists.

The film and television department of the school trains directors, cameramen, film editors, television assistants, and broadcast directors. Cameramen and directors take part in four-year day-time courses. Film editors attend special evening courses in the techniques of film editing. Assistants and broadcast directors receive professional certificates on completing their course at the school. All students at the school receive film and television training from the first semester. The school has its own four-camera television studio, in which students can obtain the necessary practical knowledge.

The Hungarian Radio and Television—within its own scope—assists in the training of mass communication specialists by providing special courses in addition to extension courses and foreign language courses.

Admission to the course for production managers is open to film and radio programme directors and university and high-school graduates. Admission is based on various selection tests. In the course for film directors one week is assigned to training in production technology, economics and finance and also labour, all subjects relevant to their work. The course for assistant directors is intended for the assistant directors and editors of radio and television and for inspectors. Admission depends on successful completion of the selection tests. The main subjects are television technology, film technology, production technology, aesthetics and studies in art, television direction, copyright regulations and psychology of art.

Extension training for journalists who have been in the profession for some time is given at the Journalists' School operated by the association and also at the Political School working in collaboration with the Central Committee of the Hungarian Socialist Workers' Party, as well as in universities and high schools.

In recent years several universities and high schools started series of lectures on various theoretical questions relating to mass communication for those working outside the system of mass communication—teachers, sociologists, politicians. The popularity of these lectures is an indication of the increased interest in the subject.

Thanks to the introduction of post-graduate training for journalists, and of organized extension training, two-thirds of those employed in mass communication now hold university or high-school degrees. The number of holders of high school diplomas is significantly higher in the age group under 40 years than in the age group over 40 years.

For 11 per cent there was a break of 5–10 years between obtaining the secondary-school certificate and starting university studies; 49 per cent held their diplomas before entering the profession, and only 15 per cent obtained them afterwards; 27 per cent of the journalists speak three or more foreign languages; 59 per cent, one or two; and a mere 14 per cent do not speak a foreign language. Attachment to their profession among those working in mass communication seems to be proved by the fact that 16 per cent state that they chose the profession before they had reached the age of 16, 45 per cent chose their profession at between 16 and 20 years of age, in 29 per cent of the cases this happened between the ages of 21 and 30 years, 6 per cent say they decided on this profession even later, and 4 per cent attribute their being in the profession to reasons independent of their decision[39].

11 Ethics, traditions

The principles of socialist mass communication are not based on abstract ideals but on a system of values which ranks the service of social interests highest. In consequence, they require unconditional respect for human rights and postulate the inviolability of the person.

Socialist society—and socialist journalism—apply legal sanctions against those who use mass media to make war propaganda, spread national, racial or religious prejudice or violate the integrity of the individual, for instance by publishing a family scandal or misusing information about the private life of a citizen.

There is no place for demagogy in mass communication; the journalist must not make impossible demands upon persons or institutions.

Mass communication must not foster or awaken illusions in the public, even if facing reality may mean social stresses.

Mass communication cannot disregard in any way the actual consequences of its activities, since it puts all its efforts and its whole mechanism at the service of socialism, which is the primary ethical value.

These norms, laid down by Lenin, regarding the general activities of mass communication do not, of course, function automatically. An extremely large number of factors determine the press morals within a society, and above all the morals of the society itself[40]. It is, however, an indisputable fact that much depends on the education and training of journalists, and a moral foundation is indispensable. In the process of socialization of the profession journalists starting their career are introduced to certain models of behaviour and moral ideals. In the programme of institutionalized training, for example, they learn about the many outstanding Hungarian politicians, writers and poets who worked as journalists for shorter or longer periods, some of whom had great influence on whole generations of journalists.

The Association of Hungarian Journalists is also concerned with regulating the behaviour of its members. The statutes of the association call for the preservation of political and moral purity in Hungarian journalism, and the progressive traditions of the profession. On the suggestion of the presidency, the board may elect as honorary member a foreign or Hungarian citizen who, in the foreign or Hungarian press, has rendered great service to the cause of peace and socialism. Members are called upon to protect carefully the good reputation of Hungarian journalists, to safeguard the principles of honesty, decency and incorruptibility among journalists.

The general meeting of the association elects, by secret ballot, an Ethical Committee consisting of nine members whose task is to observe, analyse and evaluate constantly the behaviour of journalists, from the point of view of ethics. It is an ethical offence for a journalist not to serve consistently the political power of the people and the building of socialism. It is likewise an offence to undermine the prestige of the profession by reprehensible activities or behaviour, or to mislead public opinion, either knowingly, or by negligence; to cause public scandal by bad conduct, to plagiarize, to reveal or to conceal information for personal advantage. An appeal to delay the decision of the Ethical Committee may be made to the presidency, and an appeal against the decision of the latter may be presented to the board within eight days[41].

Apart from social sanctions applied against a journalist guilty of an ethical offence, the direct editor may be obliged, by legal measures, to publish a correction if one of his contributors has published or spread untrue facts, or presented true facts in a false light.

Naturally, the ethical norms of journalism are not based primarily on codified prohibitions or possible sanctions, but upon the agreement of the individual with the moral principles originating in the social order, and the nature of his education. It is also obvious that socialist morality is not the end but the means of the mass communication system; at the same time, it makes demands upon the journalist whose personality will be formed within the framework of these demands.

12 Summary

The function of mass communication in Hungary is both political and educational; in the broadest sense it is to encourage the construction of a new type of relationship between the individual and the community. Therefore, the reflection of reality takes precedence over escape from reality, creative activity over consumer passivity, community orientation over individual isolationism, both in the form and content of communication.

Mass communication is taking a more and more central place in the life of Hungarian society, because of the ongoing process of democratization, the increasing political activity of citizens, the differentiation of their cultural demands, the rising standard of living and the extension of leisure time as well as the integration of certain elements of the scientific-technical revolution into everyday life.

The rapid development of mass communication has resulted in a transformation of the structure of the Hungarian communication system, the electronic media gaining ground to the detriment of the classic types of media, mass communication in general gaining ground at the expense of a more traditional type of transfer of information and culture. None the less the communication system has remained an integrated whole incorporating new and traditional channels alike, and both communication policies and communication plans relate to the whole of this complex system.

Communication policies reflecting the value- and norm-system of socialist society are formulated at various institutional levels, regulating communication processes by provisions of law, the adoption and application of certain principles and by economic and administrative measures. These policies constitute a more and more coherent system of regulations and they rely, to a growing extent, on complex social planning.

In the process of elaborating and implementing communication policies socialist society uses experimental methods to meet challenges without historical precedents in the domain of information and culture. Development of the communication system is an integral part of the cultural revolution which is in turn part of the political-social revolution. To quote Marx: 'The revolution of the people is total: every sphere makes its revolution in its own way; why should the press as such not do the same.'